Contents

Godzwow.

Into The Garden

Nina L. Hayden
Godzwow Publications, Inc.

Copyright

Dedication

To YHVH (Father God),

without whom I would have

never taken on this task.

I am entirely devoted to You, as

my love for You is eternal.

Endorsements

It is with pleasure that I write an endorsement for Nina's book. She has taken a concept and made it come alive in an easy way, giving the reader the chance to apprehend the immensely creative way that YHVH has made for us to be able to come into union with Him. Having walked into a relationship like this, there is no turning back.

Regards,

Ian Clayton
Son of Thunder

In this powerful book, Nina unveils the reality of who we really are not only as a believer but as a mature son. She encourages and challenges you to go beyond religion based on tradition to stepping into a real, tangible, experiential relationship with Jesus, God the Father, and Holy Spirit by desiring and going after a face to face encounter and communion with Them.

Nina continues to show you can walk out your Destiny Scroll from a deep place of intimacy. She also gives you the understanding and wisdom to mature as a Son, presenting you to the Father ready to receive and display His power, authority, and responsibility in all of creation. Nina takes you on a journey of what it means to hear the voice of the

Father and to see His face. She helps you step into the frequencies that come from His heart, which is the place where we must always operate.

As you read this book, I encourage you to let go of the things of the past, engage your spirit-man. Open up your heart to receive the new mysteries the father has prepared for such a time as this, for whosoever chooses to step into them. Allow yourself to be stretched through these powerful truths found in this book. Only through the stretching will you grow, carrying out everything that Yahweh has put inside your original Blueprint so that you can walk out your Destiny Scroll.

Nina is an incredible Son of Yahweh, walking with the love and heartbeat of Adonai, reflecting through her everywhere she goes. I am incredibly blessed to call her my sister, my friend, and a fellow co-laborer in the Kingdom Realms of our Father!

Corina Toncz-Patacki
Kingdom Reflections Inc.

For many individuals who consider themselves Christian, their position is a nominal one. Nina Hayden's book *Into the Garden* causes us to take a more in-depth look at our relationship with God. Her journey towards engagement with a Father who yearns for a relationship will help everyone who reads it, forge their path toward the Father's heart. This book is a must-read for those who crave intimacy.

Ruth Forde
Founder and President of Welborn Inc.

One of the greatest tools in the life of a believer is testimonial power. This expression of our speech creates a living testimonial atmosphere that entwines yesterday, today, and tomorrow within the reality of how the Hand and Word of God has and continues to direct our lives. Living out of the future today is strengthened by testimonial power. We allow this expression of truth to forge a reality of faith that is beyond what we can see and imagine. In her book, Nina has placed this testimonial power in the hands of believers. Through practical and straight forward language, Nina walks us through the testimonial power that has developed through her walk with God. Faith inspires faith and Hope equips us to live a life that is rich with the resources and atmosphere of our Father's House. This book will both inspire you and equip you to stand and speak aloud your own testimonial power.

Mazel tov to you, Nina, for this beautiful and honest expression of your faith, hope, and love in YHVH. It is both an honor and a privilege to know you and witness the wonder and joy of your faith.

Shalom Ahavah Simcha,

Karl Whitehead

Nina has written an outstanding book. She invites us on her journey with Yahweh and brings into play powerful principles and eternal truths that challenge and stretch us. She is an amazing woman of God who has walked through fire and testing and entered the deep heart of Yahweh. It is my honor and privilege to call her friend and sister on this journey.

Now here is her first book she is releasing to love and bless us. Read it and be transformed.

Mary Ottmann-Bass
Co-Founder and President of Shaar Lamed

We so love Nina's heart to pursue intimacy with God even when it is challenging. She shares her journey candidly to experience a God that is beyond verses on a page or words spoken from the pulpit. She carries a passion for the Father's heart, to know and be known by him – similar to one of our plumb lines, "Ask the Father." The story of her heart "transplant" will touch yours and inspire you to seek that deeper place Father has for all of us. Through the challenges of health, experiencing divorce, and even running for political office, Nina demonstrates that the love of God triumphs overall. Whatever you are faced with, her story will move and inspire you to a deeper walk with God. You will love Nina's description of the garden of her heart and be challenged to shift how you pray - to a new and living way. Don't miss this opportunity to see into the beautiful heart of God through Nina's eyes.

Gil and Adena Hodges
Kingdom Talks Media

When I first met Nina Hayden, it was in a crowded room of over 150 people, yet she stood out due to the presence of the Lord that radiated off of her life. Nina walks in a deep relationship with Yahweh and operates with authority as a son of the Living God. In her book, *Into the Garden*, Nina invites you into deeper levels of relationship with the Lord by sharing keys that have opened doors of intimacy and personal stories of her own journey. I have no doubt if you engage these tools, you too can experience the Lord in a deeper and more intimate way.

Mark Wilburn
NEOS Capital Development Group

Introduction

"Come now, and let us reason together, saith the Lord: though your sins be as scarlet, they shall be as white as snow; though they be red like crimson, they shall be as wool." (Isaiah 1:18. KJV) Through the word made flesh, the invitation is given to come, reason, commune, and walk with God. **We are not alone to fend for ourselves in this world.**

Through the sacrifice of Jesus and the gift of Holy Spirit, we can speak to our Heavenly Father as though we are talking to a friend. He can express His mysteries to us personally and through the blood of Jesus, wash us clean from every stain of sin. God yearns to have a closer walk with us, His creation. In this world, so many believe one must exhibit works before a higher power accepts them. However, it is good to know our Heavenly Father seeks to have a personal and intimate relationship with each one of us, regardless of our works or sinful nature.

This concept is challenging to grasp for those who are soon to know God. It is also just as challenging to understand for those who say they know Him. Why would a God who is all-powerful and all-knowing care about us? Why would He want to spend time and have a personal relationship with us?

Well, the simple answer is, He LOVES us. "But God commendeth his love toward us, in that, while we were yet sinners, Christ died for us." (Romans 5:8 KJV) "For God so loved the world, that he gave his only begotten Son, that whosoever believeth in him should not perish, but have everlasting life." (John 3:16 KJV) God loves us so much He sacrificed His Son for us so we could live with Him for eternity.

For some of you reading this book, this concept is not new. You already know Jesus died for you, and if you didn't know that, more than likely, you have heard it stated many times by others. Jesus' story is preached in every religion that believes in His birth, death, and resurrection. His sacrifice is a foundational principle.

However, religions today haven't moved much beyond this principle. In other words, Jesus is preached about in church, talked about in Bible study, and written about in songs that are sung in worship. Yet, little is spoken about who He is. Personal encounters with Jesus are rarely shared. Some believe it is impossible to see the face of God and live. Hmm...is that true? We will talk about that later in this book.

I believe in getting to know who Jesus is, one must do more than just hear about Him, read about Him, and sing about Him. To get to know who Jesus is, one must **encounter** Him.

Ian Clayton wonderfully describes, in many of his teachings, the Bible is a "love letter to the body of Christ." I totally agree! This love letter is the first step in revealing who Father, Son, and Holy Spirit are. It's an invitation to learn how the Father's heart works, but it doesn't tell the whole entirety of who God is.

Some feel if they have read this love letter and can quote it by memory, they have adequately and effectively reached the pinnacle of what it means to know Father, Son, and Holy Spirit. However, we can only go so deep knowing who they are if we approach the love letter this way. It would be equivalent to reading a love letter from a friend or romantic interest and not wanting to get to know who they are by seeing them in person. If we're going to know the Father, Son, and Holy Spirit at a deeper level, we must engage with and personally encounter who they are as Beings.

This book is written to inspire readers to engage with God at the deepest levels. I desire that you read this book and experience the joy that I have found encountering God in the garden of my heart. Together we can learn we were made to be and administrate God's Kingdom on earth as it is in heaven.

Chapter 1 – Created
For Intimacy

"The LORD appeared to us in the past, saying:
'I have loved you with
an everlasting love; I have drawn you with
unfailing kindness.'" (Jeremiah 31:3 NKJV)

From the beginning of our existence on this planet, when we were formed in our mother's womb, Father's intense desire was and *is* to bring us back to Himself. He formed us out of love, fashioned with the intent to complete our destiny scroll, no matter what circumstances surrounded our births. Father created us for intimacy, and His will is that we are to know Him as He knows us, so we can share the truth to the world that He is LOVE.

Many struggle with the concept God is a loving God who only seeks to do good towards humanity. They do not believe God truly loves them or wants to be involved in their daily lives. I can testify to this belief. My parents raised me as an Adventist, where they displayed the doctrines of the faith as well as anyone. My mother was loving and kind, and my father did his best to provide a home and spiritual principles for us to follow. I look back on those years with fond memories. Even though my household was not perfect, my belief in God and His love for me was sound. So, I thought...

As I began to grow in adulthood and the circumstances of life presented hardships that threatened my health, relationships, and livelihood, I began to wonder, where is God in all of this? I thought He loved me and only wanted good for my life? I can remember an instance, when I was unemployed, bills were due, and I had no idea how I was going to pay for anything. The experience was so debilitating I understand how one can get so depressed they contemplate taking their own life.

I was very angry with God, believing He left me to take care of myself, with no guidance as to how I was to move forward. This was a difficult time in my life. I was hearing from so many people telling me what to do, but I could not hear the voice of God. He was silent to me, and that was very frustrating.

One day during this experience, I was lying in bed, feeling discouraged, and deeply depressed. When I woke up a few hours later, I remember hearing a still small voice. So soft, if I hadn't been coming out of sleep, I wouldn't have heard it. The voice whispered, "*Talk to me.*" My first reaction was explosive, "Whhhaaattt! I have been talking to You for a couple of months now and haven't heard anything!" The voice didn't say anything else. But, I knew God was listening as I ranted and raved for the next few hours.

After that encounter, providence revealed

God's leading in the situation. Even though I did not hear a voice that told me exactly what to do, it did become more evident what I was supposed to do, and I knew God was leading. It was a time of great faith for me, and I had to decide to believe God loved me and commit to following Him even if I wasn't sure how things would turn out. I spent three years on that journey, where I was employed on and off with no steady income—three years of trusting Him, even though I didn't know what the end would entail.

Looking back on that experience, I can see it was a time of "growing up" for me. To be honest, before then, I had no real spiritual depth. I didn't understand God's, unconditional LOVE. It's easy to believe God loves you when things are going great in your life. Don't misunderstand, though; I had experienced struggles before. However, in this circumstance, I was tested differently. Did I believe God loved me? And, if so, did He only have good things for me?

This was a pivotal turning point in my relationship with God. In this situation, He was drawing me to Himself, letting me know who He really was. During this circumstance, I began to know Him as Father God, Abba Daddy, the One whom I could trust, instead of God. He revealed to me He was my provider, and I was to depend on no one else. I didn't realize how much I depended on voices from others or my steady income from my job. Through the experience, Daddy was able to strip away my dependence on things so that I could depend on Him for everything.

I was able to pay my rent, car note, and other bills with no job! I saw firsthand my Daddy work mightily for me, and I also realized how much He loved me! If my Father could orchestrate a circumstance in such a way to reveal to me how trustworthy He is, I knew I could depend on Him no matter what. And I knew He LOVED me! It was miraculous. I still celebrate the goodness He showed me from that situation.

Sometimes we as believers think we are going through hardship because the devil is attacking us. That could be true, but maybe it isn't. Our Father often orchestrates challenging circumstances to wake us up to the reality that He wants us to know Him as our provider and that He LOVES us. In this way, He shows us there is no other way to true peace, joy, and fulfillment than through knowing Him and trusting in Him in all things. Through these circumstances, we mature in our relationship with Him, so our foundation is rock solid, and He can trust us when He needs to use us for greater things that will bring about His glory! Come on now, testify!

"And we know that all things work together for good to those who love God, to those who are called according to His purpose." (Romans 8:28 NKJV) Encountering Abba Daddy through my life experiences, has genuinely given me a perspective regarding this verse. I can say with high confidence;

in Him, I fully trust and know He LOVES me! I know He created me for intimacy to love Him because He first loved me! By the way, it took me four decades to come to this conclusion. How about you?

Chapter 2 – Engaging Father's Heart

"Glory ye in his holy name: let the heart of them rejoice that seek the Lord." (1 Chronicles 16:10 KJV)

Engaging Father's heart is the most important action we can do as human beings on this planet. There is nothing more critical because anything done, spoken, or thought of outside of His heart will have no lasting effect in His Kingdom. This means we must know His heart in all situations. In this way, we join in partnership with Him to reveal His Kingdom on earth as it is in heaven. So, the question is, "How do we know His heart?"

The Bible says, "My sheep hear my voice, and I know them, and they follow me." (John 10:27 NKJV) Wow! This verse alone could be unpacked in a separate book with many chapters. For now, let's focus on, "My sheep hear my voice." The religious system today is set up where pastors are overworked and overwhelmed because church members inundate them with requests. Instead of Jesus being the Shepard, the one that is to teach, guide, and instruct. Religion places the pastor in the role of Shepard, causing the flock to be dependent upon him or her instead of Jesus. Church members constantly seek the pastor's advice on physical, psychological, economic, and domestic issues. The pastor is set up as the one with all of the answers. Or at least, the one who can pray to get all of the answers.

It is very dangerous when this happens. The pastor's voice becomes the voice of God and becomes the guiding factor in the individual's life. This makes it difficult for the individual to discern for him or herself what Jesus is telling them to do.

Father had to "grow me" in this area. When I was less mature in my spiritual relationship with Father, I habitually called family members and friends every time I had a major decision to make. Even when the opinions conflicted, and I felt more confused about the decision I was supposed to make after getting several opinions, I still kept doing it. Now that is the real definition of insanity!

One day, applying my usual crazy tactic to make an important decision, I decided to call my group of "advisors." As I picked up my mobile phone, I heard a voice as clear as day. I can't tell you if the voice was in my spirit or at the outside of my ear, but I can tell you, it was super clear. The voice said, *"You need to speak to Me first before you make another decision."* I remember feeling very convicted. I knew I had gotten into a habit of speaking to so many others before going to Father.

Father was the last one I got my opinions from. I'm ashamed to admit it, but it was true. I'm sure you can't relate to this feeling, or can you?

So, from that moment on, I purposed in my heart I would go to Father first when making any decision. I'm not stating you can't go to your pastor, godly family members, and friends to seek counsel. My advice would be to go to Father first; then, if you need confirmation and Father reveals to you He has a word for you through someone else, you can hear what another has to say.

I'm passionate about this topic because today, more than ever, we must learn to engage with Father's heart for ourselves. Engaging with Father's heart is the foremost way to know Him and to keep from being deceived. Yes, that's right...hearing Father for **yourself** will keep you from being deceived because you aren't dependent on someone else's opinion. This is especially true regarding the interpretation of scripture.

Religion today prescribes a set of rules, governed by a body of rule makers, whose interpretation of scripture implies infallibility. In addition, most religious teachings today are stagnant and taught out of doctrines of the past. When a person today presents a revelation of Father's heart, which seems to contradict the doctrine of the past, the person is seen as heretical or an apostate. If believers blindly follow a religion without developing a relationship with Father for themselves, they will have no firm foundation to stand upon when religion fails them, or other challenges come to test their faith.

A similar situation happened in the scriptures when a "new way" was established. The Jews who believed in Jesus were called "believers in the way." In the new way, Jews no longer had to participate in the temple sacrifice because a greater sacrifice had come, presented through the body, death, and resurrection of Jesus. The old beliefs in temple sacrifice were no longer necessary, and those who believed or taught contrary to the "old way" were deemed heretics or apostates. Those who chose to follow the new way were convicted of the message that came through the Truth, Jesus Himself. Those who chose to blindly follow the old way of sacrifice followed a path that proved fatal when the Romans later surrounded Jerusalem, and many Jews died as a result.

Father, Jesus, and Holy Spirit have no religious doctrine. They want us to know who they are beyond what religion has to offer. They have given us a love letter, the Bible, as an invitation to get to know who they are personally, and nothing in the Bible implies, a pastor, spiritual guide, evangelist, etc., can teach you about the love letter better than Holy Spirit. The Bible says, "And as for you, the anointing which ye received of him abideth in you, and ye need not that anyone teach you; but as his anointing teacheth you concerning all things, and is true, and is no lie, and even as it taught you, you abide in him." (1 John 2:27 KJV)

When individual effort is made to engage with the heart of the Father for oneself, He is known by you as you are known by Him. There is a reward for those who diligently seek Him and your heart will rejoice, because in "Him you live, and move, and have your being..." (Acts 17:28 NKJV) You will know His voice, and God will be the guiding factor leading you.

Today, Father is revealing more than He has ever before. Revelation is being given to those who are engaged with His heart and know His voice. For some, this revelation is likely outside the comfort zone and framework of what is currently being taught. The age where Daniel's book was closed has now opened. We are in a new era and Father is calling us to engage with His heart so He can show us more profound revelation. He wants us to see ourselves differently. He is calling us to see ourselves more than just His children. He is calling us to see ourselves as His Sons.

Chapter 3 – From
Children To Sons

"For the earnest expectation of creation waiteth
for the revealing of the sons of
God." (Romans 8:19 NKJV)

Father is looking for His children to become Sons. The label Son is not based on our gender in the natural world. The label Son is based on the spiritual authority Father gives us. Just as men are part of the church, which is often referred to as the Bride of Christ, women can be called Sons. Being called a Son is the desire of Father's heart so we may become mature in our relationship with Him, and He may trust us to do what He has called us to do.

Currently, Christianity is filled with Father's children. Children who have not yet matured much and are very comfortable going to church, singing praise songs, hearing a sermon, and going home unchanged in their everyday lives. His children are tethered to the things of this life and spend little time engaging in a meaningful way with Him, Jesus, or Holy Spirit. This is evident because many of His children lack supernatural power in their lives. And, when it comes to their faith being tested, there is little to stand on. They are full of fear and are no different than the world.

For example, in September of 2017, a Category 5 hurricane was set to hit the state of Florida in the southern region near the Keys and make its way through Pinellas County. I have lived in Florida since January of 1999. I have never seen a panic so profound sweep across the state. I believe the fear was compounded by the previous hurricane that had destroyed the southern portion of Texas.

There have been many hurricanes in Florida since 1999. However, it felt like September 2017 was on another level in terms of the pandemonium. The weather forecasters created so much fear you could literally feel the fright in the air. Gas was gone in a matter of hours, and police cars drove through the streets with loudspeakers calling for everyone to evacuate.

I have never been in a war situation, but it felt like my home was under siege. It seemed imminent that something harmful was about to happen. Everyone was focused on asking each other what they were going to do. Family members called to find out what my plans were for the storm. Friends and family members on Facebook, who live in the northeast part of the country, were scared for my safety.

From the beginning of the storm's forecast, I immediately went to Father to talk to Him about it. In those days, I wasn't where I am today in my Sonship journey. But, I was one who knew the voice of Father and could clearly discern what I was supposed to do. I had gone through several years of my faith being tested and was prepared to do what Father told me to do, no matter what others said or did. Hours before the storm, there were so many voices, so much commotion. Friends close to me were leaving town, they were finding refuge in any place but my county. Some stayed in the county but left their homes to find shelter in local designated areas. I chose to stay in my home because that is what Father told me to do.

This is one of those times where I was going to ride out a storm, literally, and I was at peace, knowing I had developed a relationship with Father and could clearly hear His voice. I had also learned from spiritual teachers earlier that we, as believers, have authority over the weather and are not confined to the natural world when addressing natural disasters. In this circumstance, I chose to exercise my faith and believe I had authority over the storm and knew Father would protect me.

The evening before the storm was supposed to hit; a police car came through the parking lot of my apartment complex. As the lights on the vehicle flashed red and blue, a voice came from the car speaker, "Please evacuate; the storm is approaching, and you must leave your residence now." The Governor sent the police cars out one more time to encourage everyone to leave the state. By then, most of the residents had already evacuated the complex, and it was pretty much like a ghost town.

The panic among believers and non-believers

was palpable. Many believers ran for their lives, riding as far as their gas could take them out of the state. Some took a plane out west, and some drove all the way north as far as Virginia. Some even tried to convince me to go with them. I remember asking them, "What did Father tell you about leaving?" I didn't get a response that had faith in it. They were already determined to leave.

As the storm came through, the devastation in my county was not nearly as bad as the news depicted. Many people lost power in their homes for a week or more, but my apartment complex lost no electricity. I remember watching the wind and rain come through. When the storm was over, I spoke to Father about the experience. He told me my apartment complex and the area surrounding it was protected because I chose to stay home. I could exercise authority over the area I was in because I decided to shelter in my home. Subsequently, very few trees were knocked down, there was no flooding in the area, so my car was safe, and the apartment complex had full access to electricity.

Unfortunately, those who made the drive out of the state could not say the same. Either damage was found to their home, or they were left with no electricity. Some came home to flooded homes, and many were caught in significant delays getting back as it was difficult to find gas when they drove through the southern states to get home. It ended up being more of a hassle for the people who left than for the people who stayed.

I learned from this experience that so many of Father's children need to mature. Being tested in a hurricane is only one test out of many a child of Father will go through on this earth. I'm sure you know that well. We are tested in our finances, relationships, health situations, pandemics, et cetera.

On my Sonship journey, I purposed to engage with the Spirit of Wisdom regarding what would be the best way to help Christians judge their spiritual walk with Father, so they intentionally make the decision to mature. The Spirit of Wisdom and I resolved four stages reveal how one *may* mature spiritually. I say *may* because spiritual maturity is a choice that must be made by the believer.

Salvation **Stage** – This is the first stage in our spiritual walk. When we are born again, we acknowledge Father, Jesus, and Holy Spirit are living inside of us. "Know ye not that ye are a temple of God, and that the Spirit of God dwelleth in you?" (1 Corinthians 3:16 KJV) We accept the sacrifice of Jesus with the belief that He died for our sins so we may live eternally. We also accept the fact that we are a new creature, and old things have passed away. This is the stage of a newborn baby. In this stage, we are learning how to crawl. We go to Daddy with our arms open wide, expecting Him to give us everything we request. Our highest concern is that all of our needs are met.

Sanctification **Stage** – In the second stage, we walk out our salvation with fear and trembling. Meaning, now we are born again, it's time to work on the temple – our body, soul, and spirit, that it may be an acceptable offering to Father. This is the stage where we are to die to self. Then Jesus told his disciples, "If anyone would come after me, let him deny himself and take up his cross and follow me." (Matthew 16:24 NKJV) In this stage, we are to pursue holiness, clean out the junk in our hearts, and turn the intent of our hearts and thoughts on our Father. We are to be in the world and not of it. The desire to want to develop a closer walk with Father is our focus. This is the stage of a teenager. We are learning to relinquish control and trust Father with control over every aspect of our lives.

Application **Stage** – In the third stage, the believer is just beginning to mature. While the believer has committed to pursuing a life of holiness and begins to incorporate into daily life a commitment to put Father first in all things, the believer also begins to apply and function in ALL of the promises of the Bible. This includes, but is not limited to, applying and functioning in love (the fruit of the Spirit) which brings joy, peace, patience, kindness, goodness, faithfulness, gentleness, and self-control. As well as applying and functioning in the gifts of the spirit – words of wisdom, words of knowledge, increased faith, gifts of healing and miracles, the gift of prophecy, discernment of spirits, speaking in tongues, and interpretation of tongues. This is the stage of a young adult. You not only speak of the Father's promises in His word you live them.

Revelation Stage – In the fourth and final stage, the believer has grown to a level of spiritual maturity where Father, Jesus, and Holy Spirit can speak mysteries to the believer personally. The believer is functioning in a position where Father trusts the believer with revelation that can be facilitated and administrated on earth. In this stage, there is such an intimate walk with Father, Jesus and Holy Spirit; the believer's intent is only to reveal Father's heart to a dying world. This is the stage of an Adult who matures into a Son.

All of these stages reflect a period in one's spiritual maturity that can easily be marked or defined. Some believers are in two or more stages at the same time. I don't believe there is a prescribed way to pass through these stages. However, one should be able to clearly define whether or not they have entered one stage or the next.

When I was in Adventism, I taught a young adult Sabbath school class. We spoke about the different stages. I asked them where they thought they were in their spiritual stage of maturity. Many of them felt they were still in the Salvation stage. Some were trying to function in the Sanctification stage but had gotten little guidance on how they were supposed to navigate that stage. There was little talk about the Application stage, especially as applied to the gifts of the spirit. And, no one even knew what the Revelation stage implied.

Since they were in the Salvation stage and struggling with the Sanctification stage, we focused on those two stages. Many struggled giving up their needs and desires to Jesus to allow the needs and desires of Father to take precedent. They spoke about being distracted with the things of this life, which made it difficult to spend time with Father. It was interesting to talk about the struggle of handing one's own desires over to Father. I enjoyed discussing the issue with young adults.

However, I don't think this struggle is specific to young people. I believe many adults struggle with the same issues. Many adults are distracted with the things of this world, and little effort is made to spend time with Father for more than a few minutes a day. This fact makes itself evident when Christians and Christian leaders consistently fall into sin.

For example, have you ever witnessed a ministry leader who moves in healing, signs, and wonders, curse like a sailor, or be unfaithful to their spouse? It gives the world a negative view of Christianity, and it bears false witness to who Father is. I'm not saying leaders or non-leaders have to be perfect as they mature. But, if we understand how to live a life of holiness, a transformation in our character will result, and sin will no longer be attractive or habitual for us.

Holiness is a result that comes out of the Sanctification stage, and I do suggest it's important to engage with the Sanctification stage before the Application or Revelation stages. The Sanctification stage is a foundational stage that ensures whatever develops and matures in the Application stage, reveals the heart of Father, and is not displayed out of the heart of man. It serves as a building block of the other stages and serves as a safeguard against a believer falling into repetitive sin. The Sanctification Stage entails cleaning out the junk inside our soul!

I'm not going to go through what it means to do that in this book. A good book you can read to help you do this is called "Gateways of the Threefold Nature of Man." It's written by Ian Clayton and has examples of his journey. This will help any believer grow in the Sanctification process and begin to know Father's heart like never before. This stage is pivotal to grow from a Child to a Son. Father cannot trust you as a Son if you do not display His character.

So, what does it mean to be a Son? The Bible has many verses that refer to us as Sons and Heirs to Father. "For as many that are lead by the Spirit of God, these are the sons of God." (Romans 8:14 NKJV) The Bible verse goes on to say we are not only children of God; we are Heirs and even so joint-Heirs with Christ. What a powerful statement! Do you consider yourself a joint-Heir with Christ? Meaning everything He has access to, so do you? If you don't believe that, then you are living like a child and not a Son.

Living the life of a Son means you have moved through the stages of spiritual maturity where you can be trusted with revelations from Father. It means you have moved from the Salvation stage where you only talk to Him when you're in a crisis or need something to setting aside meaningful time every day to converse with Father just to get to know His heart. As a Son, the intent of your heart is turned toward the Father. Everything you do is out of holiness. When you understand how to deal with sin in your life and work on it until it no longer has a hold on you, walking in holiness is not a struggle.

Sonship involves displaying the fruit of the Spirit (love) so you no longer walk in fear of anything. It is evident you are a Son by the words you speak because you realize you frame the world around you to life or death. You walk in the promises of Father and know His word is truth because you realize you have authority over sickness, disasters, and death. Most importantly, being a Son means you are walking in your destiny on earth and in heaven. Father has spoken His mysteries to you personally and is teaching you how to administrate His will on earth and everywhere else creation groans.

With that being said, I'm not sure why anyone would pass up Father's calling to Sonship (spiritual maturity). The journey does take time and intentionality, but the rewards of being a Son outweighs anything the world has to offer. I'm hoping you'll join me on this journey. In fact, Father is calling you to Sonship. Will you accept?

Chapter 4 – A Heart Of Flesh

"A new heart also will I give you, and a new spirit
will I put within you: and I will take
away the stony heart out,
of your flesh, and I will give you an heart
of flesh." (Ezekiel 36:26 KJV)

In Chapter 2, we discussed the importance of engaging Father's heart. The Bible tells us, out of the heart the mouth speaks. If our hearts are full of His love, we will say what Father says. Our thoughts will be His thoughts, and our actions will reflect the actions of the Kingdom. However, if our hearts are hard, broken, and hurting, it will be clear in our actions and words we have issues that need to be dealt with. It will also be difficult to connect with Father's heart because our hearts have created barriers that prevent deep intimacy.

The most important aspect I have noticed on this journey is how difficult it is for Christians to connect to Father's heart. Through heartbreak, trauma, or simply putting their desires above Father, their hearts have grown stony, and the heart of flesh Father purposed for them is no longer available. The interesting thing is, many believers don't even know they have a stony heart until they decide to connect more intimately with Father.

There were a couple of circumstances that affected my heart. As a child, I had a deep love for Father. I grew up in a spiritual household. My father pastored a church, and my mother lead out in women's ministries. My siblings and I were close, and I had friends from church and school that were as close as family. I will never forget the day I was baptized. I was 12 years old and could feel the presence of Holy Spirit so strongly...it was tangible. However, as I grew older, my desire for the world became stronger than my desire for Father, and I made many decisions that took my heart away from Him. That might sound pretty surprising for a pastor's daughter, right? Ha! Ha!

You hear it all the time, "...pastor's kids are the wildest children out there." Well, there is some merit to that. It was common for me to be out clubbing one night and in church singing praise songs while hungover the next morning. I had one foot in the church and one foot in the world. I didn't consider if Father loved me, or if I loved Him. I felt He was there but didn't spend much time getting to know Him because my focus was more on having fun and enjoying life. You could say my love for Him grew cold, and my heart was focused on my own desires. It was difficult for me to hear His voice because I didn't spend the time to learn to recognize it.

It wasn't until I left my hometown to go to law school in Florida that my spiritual life became more real. I was fortunate to be surrounded by people who sincerely wanted to know who Father was. I was tired of doing my own thing and knew there was much more to life than just partying. I knew my heart had grown cold, and I wanted to change that, so I purposed to seek Father's heart. My desire was to get back to the first love I had for Father when I was a child. However, another situation occurred, which made it difficult for me to connect with Father.

When I moved to Florida, I was married. My husband and I met when we both lived in Maryland, and our fathers pastored different churches. We were best friends and had a lot in common. We went to the same high school and dated for a couple of years before we got married. The beginning of our marriage was pretty uneventful. We deeply loved each other and were known for how affectionate we were when we were together. He used to leave love notes for me to read when he left for work.

After a year and a half into the marriage, I began to have health problems. So much to the point that I couldn't function with the same energy I had before. Law school was becoming more difficult to keep up with, and I didn't have the slightest clue why I was feeling the way I was. My husband was very supportive of my care and did what he could to help.

We tried to figure out what was going on. I went to doctor after doctor but could not get a diagnosis as to what was happening to me. All I knew is that I didn't feel well and didn't know if I would have the stamina to complete the semester in law school. I remember trying to complete a final exam in the summer semester. By the time I took the exam, I was in a wheelchair. I could hardly focus, and I told the Dean of the law school I didn't think I could complete the semester. I lost the entire semester that summer and eventually had to re-take the same amount of credits, two years later.

During this time, my husband and I had to make a serious decision. My health was failing to the point he couldn't take care of me by himself, so we decided to move back to Maryland to live with my parents. I had to take a leave of absence from law school, and I wasn't sure if I was going to return.

My health challenges were a tremendous test for our marriage. We lasted for another two years, just enough time for me to get better and re-enter law school, but by the middle of the next year, we were divorced. It was a painful period in my life. Even though I had strengthened my spiritual walk with Father, the brokenness my heart felt from the divorce was very difficult to bear, and it made it difficult to feel Father's presence.

As time went by, I found myself in deep sorrow now and then over the divorce. One day while driving in the car, going through one of those moments, I was fed up with feeling that way and just couldn't take it anymore. So, I cried out, "JESUS, PLEASE GIVE ME A NEW HEART!" I was in tears and wanted my heart to be whole again.

The next morning as I was waking out of sleep, a vision of Jesus flashed in front of me. Jesus took his hand, reached into my chest, and took my heart out of me. Then He reached His hand into His own chest, took out his heart, and put it in my chest. From that point on, as Jesus is my witness, the sorrow was completely gone, and my heart was whole. I could love deeply again, totally and completely with trust and no fear.

It was an amazing miraculous experience, and I have no hesitation telling people about it! There is truth to the verse that says, "So if the Son sets you free, you will be free indeed." (John 8:36 NIV) You see, Father wants us all to be free. Free to love Him with all of our heart so we can love others with all of our heart. This is the purpose of love, to be so entwined with Father's love that we are to "become love," as Nancy Coen stated at her Quantum Shift #5 Conference. Isn't that powerful! Since we as a body of believers are purposed to shift this planet in a way that will change creation's destiny, we must commit to being Sons who *are* love, so ALL of creation will know us *as* love!

If you desire intimacy with Father, Jesus, and Holy Spirit but have a heart that is hurt, broken, or has drifted away, I encourage you to ask Him for a new heart. If He did it for me, He will do it for you. He wants to connect with you in an intimate way so you will know the plans He has for you. He may miraculously give you a new heart right away, or He may lead you and show you what you need to do to break down the barriers of your heart, so you are freely able to connect with Him. Whatever the case may be, He will help you, and it will happen. I can tell you because I know my Daddy and I know His love never fails!

Chapter 5 – Three But One

"That they all may be one; as thou,
Father art in me, and I
in thee, that they also may be one in
us..." (John 17:21 KJV)

Father, Jesus, and Holy Spirit intend that we be one in Them. They are three in one, and we are to be one in them, moving, living, and breathing. For some, this may be difficult to grasp. Even some mature believers don't understand this concept. They aren't clear regarding the role of the Godhead and how we are to engage with each of Them.

I believe this topic underscores the point made in the introduction that reading the love letter (the Bible) is not enough. To know who Father, Jesus, and Holy Spirit are, we must engage with Them. One encounter with Them will change your life, and as you begin to connect with each of them separately, you'll get a better understanding of who They are.

The following is a brief account of how I came to know Them. I'm hoping you can relate to some of what I have experienced. If not, I know this will encourage you to have a relationship with Them for yourself. For there is nothing more fulfilling in this world than to know where you have come from and who you belong to.

Holy Spirit (Ruach Hakodesh), Helper, Comforter, Guide and Best Friend – I'm not sure how I could have survived without Holy Spirit, The One I love more than anything. My first experience getting to know Holy Spirit started right before I got sick. I was in the beginning of my second year of law school and was working at the Gap, a clothing store, in the mall near my house. At the time my husband and I were seeking The Lord, wanting a closer relationship with Him. One day I was driving home from work heading to my house. I was singing, praising The Lord when an outpouring of the presence of Holy Spirit came upon me like a flood. I had never felt that before and was so filled with joy.

It was similar to what I felt when I got baptized but 10 times more intense. I didn't understand at the time that what I felt was Holy Spirit's way of preparing me for what I was about to through with my health. From that time on, I was drawn to Holy Spirit. I felt Holy Spirit near me in such an intense way I began to connect deeper. Holy Spirit was The One I began to lean on. I felt comforted that when I connected with Holy Spirit, I could feel a heavenly presence. Whenever I had a question, I would go to Holy Spirit in the middle of my heart and ask. At that time, instead of hearing a voice, divine providence would clearly show me the answer.

Holy Spirit also communicated with me in

other ways. Pictures would flash in my mind when we spoke. I would a see picture of where I lost my keys. A picture warning me not to forget a computer cord when I needed it. Or, a picture to remind me to call a person or do a task I had forgotten to do. It was amazing that we had encounters so often. Holy Spirit became real to me and became my best friend.

My relationship with Holy Spirit strengthened even more, when I was forced to return to my parents' house because of my health. I was 26 years old. For the first 16 weeks, I laid in the bed on my back, unable to move. I couldn't sit up and could not feed myself. My husband had to pick me up and carry me to the bathroom for a bath, and my family took turns bringing the bedpan in the room for me to use the bathroom. It was a humbling and challenging experience.

For those four months, when I was on my back in the bed, I spent most of the time talking to Holy Spirit. I didn't speak out loud; I spoke to Holy Spirit in the center of my heart. I only got a couple of hours of sleep a day, and I remember being awake most nights. All I did every night was talk to Holy Spirit. I'm surprised Holy Spirit wasn't tired of hearing me talk. We talked about anything and everything for hours.

When I think about it today, the experience was surreal. While my body was wrecked in excruciating pain, I was with my Best Friend and had no doubt Holy Spirit was there. It took me two years to recover from whatever happened to my body. After regaining the strength to walk again and feed myself, I was able to re-enter law school, complete the course requirements, and earn a degree.

During this journey, I finally began to recognize the voice of Holy Spirit. It was a still small voice that came from inside me. I wondered why I hadn't noticed it before. I think it was because my thoughts were loud and needed to be silent long enough so I could recognize a voice. I have had so many encounters with Holy Spirit; I could write many books about them. And I'm proud to say Holy Spirit is my everlasting love, and each experience I have gone through has solidified that even more.

Now, I'm not implying you have to go through such a dramatic situation as I did to hear Holy Spirit's voice. However, I can say, if you want to hear Holy Spirit you must set aside time, be still, wait and listen. Holy Spirit will speak to you. I guarantee it!

Jesus (Yeshua/YHSVH), Savior, Warrior, Older Brother, and Love – Jesus is my amazing example. I love Him with all of my being. I first learned about Him as a child. My mother and father instilled in me the sacrifice He made for me when He died on the cross. But when I was younger, I connected with Him half-heartedly and didn't begin to call on Him or talk to Him until I became older and had challenges in my life.

When I first began to talk to Him, I was older, going through circumstances I knew He could relate to.

After all, He walked on this earth as a human, and the Bible says He was tempted in all ways like we are. So, when temptations came in my life, I would specifically call on Him to help me overcome.

I also looked to Jesus as an example to follow in the way I treated others, and others treated me. The Bible says He was despised and rejected, and we read even the ones that were closest to Him betrayed Him. Yet, in all of that abuse, He did not open His mouth or say a word. What a Warrior! I so admire the way He lived on this planet, and I used His example as a guiding light for me.

I can specifically point to when I first ran for political office. It was a real test for who I was as a believer. I had to come to terms with how I was going to keep to my convictions while engaging in the election process. Barack Obama was running for President for the first time when I ran for the Pinellas County School Board in 2008. My race was an at-large race. Approximately 900,000 registered voters in the county were able to take part in the election.

I had no clue what I was in for. I hadn't been involved in politics as a candidate before and was new to the entire process. It was a real challenge in many ways. The pressure of having to be at so many events, traveling all over the county, and being judged by the amount of money you could raise was a lot to handle at times. Even for a person who enjoys connecting with people and talking about issues that matter most to them, it tested me more than I bargained for.

I remember being confronted with people who didn't like me. They didn't like what I stood for because I didn't believe the same way they did. I remember receiving an e-mail from an individual who proceeded to tell me who I was and where I should go. Let's just say it wasn't friendly by any means. It would have been easy for me to be hurt and/or offended. In fact, I was very tempted to go in that direction, but I choose instead to forgive them and love them in my heart. I wrote back to this person and said, "I'm sorry we don't believe the same way, and I wish you well."

That wasn't the first incident of choosing not to get offended. There were many times I had to read criticism about myself in newsprint and online. The media spoke negatively about my website, my political platform, and distorted statements made during phone interviews. Needless to say, I had to learn to stay true to who I was as a follower of Jesus or be consumed by the negativity that surrounded the political process. I learned from that experience to be "unoffendable." People will say things that are not nice, and treat you in hurtful ways, only you are responsible for the way you respond.

I decided I was not going to be identified by what people say. I looked to Jesus, who gave me comfort. If He could love people despite the way He was treated, so could I. That was the very beginning of my getting to know Him as an Older Brother and

Warrior. My relationship with Him now has grown much deeper than that. Jesus is more real to me than just relating to Him as a Savior, Brother, and Warrior. Today, He is my love and friend. I will talk more about that later in this book.

Father God (Yahweh/YHVH), Abba, Protector, and First Love – My Daddy is incredible, and my love for Him deeper than I can express. Yet, it wasn't always that way. Today, He is first and foremost at the center of the love gate of my heart, and now I make sure what I'm doing or saying reflects His heart.

In the past, the extent of my relationship with Him centered around asking Him for things. Yes, I was one of those believers who went to Daddy only when I needed something. I also used to fast (give up food), so Daddy would see I was suffering, be proud of me, and give me what I was requesting. Wow! What an immature way of engaging with Father. However, that's where I was, and Father in His goodness directed me through His providence to show me His will for my life. He knew there would come a day when our relationship would grow, and He could teach me a more mature way to connect with Him.

I remember one circumstance where I asked; actually, I begged, Abba Daddy for a specific place I wanted to purchase as my home. It looked great on the inside when I first looked at it. I set my heart upon this place and asked Abba Daddy over and over again to give it to me. In His patience and goodness, He did. But, when I moved in, I realized the place wasn't as nice as I thought it was. It had internal problems I had to deal with, and soon one thing after the other broke down. I also had to deal with an invasion of various insects, which isn't uncommon in Florida; however, this was worse than most.

In the end, I regretted purchasing the place and wondered why Father had given me the place when He knew it had all of these problems. When I asked Him, He told me He gave it to me because I asked for it. "Hmmm...," I thought. "Well, that's true." From that moment on, I was more careful with what I asked Father to give me. I realized He is so good He will give you what you ask for, even when it isn't the best for you.

This revelation showed me how patient He is. He is willing to wait until we are ready to admit we are tired of leading our own lives and are willing to let Him lead us. From that circumstance, I learned I should consult Father first before asking for things or doing things in the future. That conscious decision changed our relationship. Instead of being Daddy that I only came to because I wanted something from Him, I began to see Him as my Father, who I came to for counsel and to see what was on His mind.

I'm sure He was happy when I finally came to that conclusion. In fact, I know He was happy because He let me know it. I also realized how happy I was giving control of my life over to Him. It was awesome knowing I was in the palm of His hand, and He was directing and guiding my life. But Father did not allow me to stay at this beginning stage of our relationship.

As soon as He saw I was willing to allow Him to lead, the tests came. He let me go through a season of tests to mature me in my love for Him. The maturing process was not so I could show Father that I love Him. The maturing process was for me to get a revelation of where my heart was in connection with His heart. Trials are totally about maturing the heart.

You see, the Bible tells us whom Father loves He corrects. I have been corrected many times, and Father knows the correction only has to come once. So, when it does, I immediately repent because the desire of my heart is to always be in line with the desire of His heart.

I want to be so in sync with His heart, I am a living, walking example of who He is. For that reason, I have made an intentional decision to get to know who Father, Jesus, and Holy Spirit are. The accounts I have just spoken about are only the beginning of the relationship I have with the Godhead. I learned to recognize each of Their voices separately, and sometimes I would speak to all three of Them at the same time.

Through my interactions with Them, I began to realize how They are Three but One. They can operate separate from each other and also together by Jesus and Holy Spirit stepping inside of Father to merge as One. Their desire is that we are one in them as they are one in each other, and They live on the inside of us for us to have access to whenever we choose. Isn't it amazing how Father created us to have God living on the inside of us! Hashilush Hakodesh (Holy Trinity) wants to have a relationship with us. They want us to know They are invested in our lives. They have an open invitation for us to participate with Them to bring about the redemption of all creation. Yay Hashilush Hakodesh! Isn't that awesome? I'm super excited about that, aren't you?

Chapter 6 – Committed

"Therefore know that the Lord your God, He is God
The faithful God who keeps
covenant...." (Deuteronomy 7:9 NKJV)

The Bible is full of verses that tell us God wants a relationship with us. So much so, He is willing to commit Himself to do it. If you haven't read about it, I encourage you to do a Bible search on the word covenant. You will see the covenant He swore to Abraham, having no name greater than His own name. He swore by His own name. Now that's a powerful covenant. (Hebrews 6:13 NKJV)

However, as believers, I don't think we understand God wants **us** to be a part of the covenant process. In other words, He not only wants us to commit to Him about what we should do. He also wants us to hold Him accountable for what we want Him to do for us. Now, this may be a stretch for some of you, because we are given the impression God wants us to obey with no dialogue regarding what that means or how that should happen. That is not the relationship He wants with His Sons. If you believe all God wants is your obedience and commitment to do what He asks, you have the mindset of a child, not a Son.

The Bible reveals a good example of this when

God delivered the Ten Commandments to Moses on the mountain of Sinai. However, before I expound on this example, let's first get some background regarding how the Jews understood creating a covenant. We can find an example of a Jewish covenant in the marriage commitment of a man and woman. The following only highlights the process of the Ketubah. If you want a more detailed description, you can purchase the teaching, "Our Ketubah with God" by Ian Clayton.

When the Jewish man makes his intentions known that he wants to make a woman his own, his treasured possession, he lets her know it's time for her to get ready to be married. Then both man and woman meet with their parents to write out the Ketubah (marriage contract).

The Ketubah is a covenant that can strictly be enforced during the marriage if one spouse is not fulfilling the terms of the contract. Thus, much thought is put into what each spouse would like, and there must be total agreement on the terms. If there is no agreement with the terms presented, both the man and woman are free to walk away from the marriage process. If there is an agreement, the ceremony is performed under the Chuppah (canopy).

In Exodus 20, we are presented with God wanting to covenant with the Jews. God has already told them He wants them for His own, His treasured possession. In anticipation of marriage, He told them to sanctify themselves to be ready to meet with Him. To finalize the marriage, a Ketubah was to be created where they could hold each other accountable, and then he would be their Chuppah (covering) all the days of their lives.

The Ketubah God wanted, and still wants to make with His people, is the Ten Commandments. Often times, we look at the Ten Commandments as something we should do. We overlook the context in which the Ten Commandments were presented because we don't study the Jewish culture to understand how God communicated with His chosen people (His bride). God's original intention was to make an individual covenant with each of the people present that day at Mount Sinai. Because they were not ready to receive God's commitment to contract individually, Moses had to engage with God on behalf of the people and receive what God had for them.

Today, that paradigm has shifted. God wants to connect with each one of us individually. He does not want a man or woman standing in relationship between us. His invitation to be married to Him still stands, and He is looking for us to participate in the Ketubah that was presented at Mount Sinai so we can hold each other accountable. There must be two participants for the marriage covenant to be complete.

After listening to the teaching by Ian Clayton I thought about what my contract terms would be to complete the Ketubah with God. I wanted to be 100% committed to Him. I also wanted to let Him know what I was expecting of Him so the Ketubah would be complete. Before writing my expectations, I also asked Father if He would like to add anything else to our Ketubah than was originally spoken on Mount Sinai. He told me what He would like included, and I added it. The following is the Ketubah I drafted. His contract terms are in **bold**, and mine are in *italic* script.

Yahweh *and Nina's* **Marriage Contract**
I am the Lord thy God, which have brought you out of the land of Egypt, out of the house of bondage. *I am your servant, daughter, best friend, and love, who lived on the stones of fire before You breathed Your breath of life into my human form, and I became a living soul.* **You shall have no other gods before me.** *I expect that You will always be there for me. When I turn my heart towards You to engage Your presence, You will always be there.* **You shall not make unto yourself any graven image, or any likeness of any thing that is in heaven above, or that is in the earth beneath, or that is in the water under the earth:** *You will change my DNA to be just like yours. You will make my heart like Yours, that I will see what You see, say what You say, and do what You do.* **You shall not bow down yourself to them, or serve them: for I the Lord thy God am a jealous God, visiting the iniquity of the fathers upon the children unto the third and fourth generation of them that hate me; And shewing mercy unto thousands of them that love me, and keep my commandments.** *You will give me your Seven Spirits*

to guide and teach me so I may truly know You and be presented before You today, ready to perform Your will on earth. **You shall not take the name of the Lord thy God in vain; for the Lord will not hold him guiltless that taketh his name in vain.** *You will help me fulfill the full potential You have ordained in my life.* **Remember the sabbath day, to keep it holy. Six days shall you labor, and do all your work: But the seventh day is the sabbath of the Lord thy God:** *When there is a task that I can do for You, You will call upon me to do it. If You would like my opinion about something You plan to do, You will call on me, and I will give it.* **In it you shall not do any work, you, your son, daughter, manservant, maidservant, cattle, and stranger that is within your gates:** *Your power will work through me, in miraculous ways to save souls for Your Kingdom.* **For in six days the Lord made heaven and earth, the sea, and all that in them is, and rested the seventh day: wherefore the Lord blessed the sabbath day, and hallowed it.** *You will keep me and protect me and my generations from any deception, attacks, or plans from evil. We will always win against evil.* **Honor thy father and thy mother: that your days may be long upon the land which the Lord thy God gives you.** *You will love me forever, tell me the desires of Your heart, and tell me the things that make You happy.* **You shall not kill.** *You will fulfill the desires of my heart when they are in line with Your perfect will.* **You shall not commit adultery.** *You will always talk to me and take time to commune with me in our secret place. You will snuggle with me.* **You shall not bear false wit-**

ness against thy neighbor. *You will talk to me face to face and discuss with me Your plans for my life, my generations, and what Your will is for us to do in the existence that always was, is and will be.* **You shall not covet thy neighbor's house, thy neighbor's husband, nor manservant, nor maidservant, nor his ox, nor his ass, nor any thing that is thy neighbor's."** *You will be my best friend, my desire, my love, and You will dance with me and sing over me.* **I can count on you when I need you, and you will always be there for Me. You will love Me always, and never forget that I love you.** *When my time on earth is done, You will translate me to heaven without seeing death and bring me to Yourself.*

This contract "sealed the deal" regarding my relationship with Father. I began to know him as Yahweh (YHVH) and have called Him by that name ever since. He has become more than just a Father to me. He has become the all-encompassing Being of eternity and beyond. For everything that was ever made in this realm and beyond is in Him, and there are so many mysteries yet to be revealed. As I have connected my heart to His, He is my covering; revealer of what He has written on my earthly and heavenly scroll, and I am committed to Him indefinitely.

In my studying of the Jewish culture, I also came to know Jesus as Yeshua (YHSVH). I learned about the culture of the Rabbis and how their students would yoke themselves to them until they

walked with the same gait, had the same mannerisms, and spoke the same way. They were committed to learning from the specific Rabbi they yoked
themselves to and would often be recognized by the
same mannerisms as the Rabbi.

Isn't that an amazing way to show one's de-
votion to another? Yeshua is our Rabbi, not only
showing us a way to Yahweh but sacrificing His life
to be the gateway back to eternity. So, in the same
way, those under to tutelage of Rabbi's yoked themselves, I have also yoked myself to Yeshua. I want to
walk the same way, speak the same way, and live the
same way He lived. I have committed myself under
His teachings and have given Him total control as
Lord, Priest, and King over my life.

In a similar way, I have made a commitment
to Holy Spirit, who I now call Ruach Hakodesh. The
Bible tells us Ruach Hakodesh was sent by Yeshua
after He returned to Heaven upon His resurrection.
Ruach Hakodesh is the very air that I breathe, and
I have bound myself in covenant. Ruach Hakodesh
resides in my being, leading and guiding me, as I fulfill my destiny scrolls.

I have written out each covenant and signed
it with Hashilush Hakodesh. It is a serious commitment. Now that I have made these commitments,
I am now held accountable for what I have written. That means I can be corrected by Hashilush
Hakodesh whenever They feel I have stepped outside of the covenants. Conversely, I can hold Them
accountable to the covenants. I know Hashilush

Hakodesh loves that we have grown into a relationship where we both can interact on these terms.

I want to encourage you to consider writing a Ketubah of your own. If you do, don't rush to do it. Take the time to think about it and dialogue with Yahweh. Better yet, use your sanctified imagination to envision what the scene looked like on Mount Sinai. Imagine yourself there with Yahweh Himself, and He is looking at you, waiting for you to let Him know what you require of Him. If you need help imagining what He looks like, read the verses in Revelation 4. You will find it's easier than you think. You will hear and see what Yahweh has to share with you.

Chapter 7 – Seeing

*"Blessed are the pure in heart for they shall
see God." (Matthew 5:8 NKJV)*

In Chapter 6, I talk about using your sanctified
imagination to engage with Yahweh. I have heard
many people say you cannot see God and live. Perhaps this is said because John 6:46 NKJV says, "...no
one has seen the Father." Yet, the Bible shows us
in Revelation 4 KJV, John does see Yahweh and also
sees Yeshua the Lamb. We also read in Exodus 33:20
NKJV, where Yeshua says, "....no man can see me and
live." Yet, Exodus 33:11 NKJV says, Moses (Moshe)
spoke to Yahweh face to face as one speaks to a
friend." These Bible verses seemingly contradict
one another and could be a little confusing for those
wanting to connect with Yahweh at a deeper level.
Perhaps we need some perspective regarding these
passages so we may engage with Hashilush Hakodesh without fear.

Let's address the Bible verse in John, where
he states no man has seen the Father. First, John is
speaking prior to his encounter with Yahweh in the
heavenlies. So, his assumption that no man has seen
the Father could have based upon his lack of experience seeing the Father. Second, when John makes
the statement, he does not qualify whether he is

speaking about a man who is pure in heart or a man who is defiled by sin. This is important because Yeshua says in Matthew 5:8 NKJV, "...one *can* see God if one is *pure in heart*."

The definition of purity is "freedom from anything that debases, contaminates, pollutes, et cetera." Once we have received Yeshua's sacrifice, we are cleansed by His blood, which serves as a gateway to enter into the purity of Yahweh's Kingdom. We can engage Yahweh in His heavenly realms and see Him. Purity of heart does not come from our own efforts. It is a gift from Yeshua, so we can connect with Yahweh how we were meant to connect before sin entered the earth.

Third, in John's statement, he does not expose as to whether or not man sees Yahweh on earth or in the heavenlies. I believe it poses more of a challenge for man to see Yahweh on earth than in heaven. The atmosphere on earth is full of sin. Yahweh would have to conceal Himself to inhabit this place. Also, most of humankind is not in a position to see Yahweh on earth because their hearts are not in a condition to receive Him.

We sing songs asking Hashilush Hakodesh to come down and fill our places of worship, yet we live our lives setting aside little time to commune with Him. I'm not saying Hashilush Hakodesh will never show Themselves on the earth. They can do whatever They want to do. Some have been very fortunate to see Them while they are on earth. However, Hashilush Hakodesh wants us to ascend to heaven to see Them, where They dwell to experience what has been purposed for us to do on earth as it is in heaven.

I have not personally seen Yahweh here on earth. Yet, I can tell you about an encounter that allowed me to see Yahweh sitting on His throne while I was in the natural realm here on earth. In the late-night hours, it is common for me to praise and worship while I'm home. I sometimes invite Yeshua to dance with me. I enjoy spending time with Him this way. He is an excellent dancer too! On one particular night, I was dancing by myself having the best time when my living room ceiling opened up on the left side. As I looked up, I saw Yahweh sitting on His throne. He was leaning over, looking down while I was dancing. He nudged Yeshua, who was sitting to the right of him and thought, "look at My daughter praising and worshipping." I could see Yahweh with His crown on His head and Yeshua sitting next to Him very pleased. It was an amazing experience! I didn't know it was going to happen. I was totally astonished when it did.

This was an amazing experience, but I want to connect with Yahweh every day. Not just an encounter here or there. When we ascend to heaven, we can have encounters with Hashilush Hakodesh every day! By ascending, we are in a place without sin, made whole by the blood of Yeshua, and can see Yahweh face to face. This is the privilege of believing in Yeshua's sacrifice and His blood. When Yeshua died on the cross, He created the gateway that allows us entry into the heavenly realms, and this is not a place we have to wait to go to after we die. We can access heaven now, as a living believer, not just when we die, and see Hashilush Hakodesh face to face!

Next, let's address the Bible verse where Yeshua said, "...no man can see *my face* and live." (Exodus 33:20 NKJV) Some people use this verse as an example of how it's impossible to see Yahweh and live. However, Exodus 33:11 NKJV tells us... "the Lord spoke to Moses face to face, as a man speaks to his friend," and we know Moshe lived.

In the first instance, Moshe had an intimate relationship with Yahweh and spoke to Yahweh as He descended in a cloud. In the second instance, Moshe asked to see Yahweh's glory, *the fullness of who Yahweh was* when Moshe was on the earth. But his physical form could not handle the fullness of Yahweh so he was sheltered in a rock.

These verses again reveal to us how important it is to engage with Yahweh not only on earth but in heaven. Why? Because when we choose to connect with Yahweh from the earth, He has to cover Himself so we may see Him. However, when we choose to ascend to heaven to connect with Yahweh, we can see the fullness of His glory in a realm where we have been washed clean by the blood of Yeshua.

My hope is that you want to see Yahweh face to face, for He is waiting for you to engage with Him. He wants you to see Him, to ascend to heaven, and gain an understanding of what He is doing on the earth and throughout all of creation.

Whether Hashilush Hakodesh chooses to present Themselves to you on earth, or in heaven, the invitation is given to *"come and see"* what They have for you. I want to encourage you to engage with Them and see what happens. If you choose to do so, I guarantee your life will never be the same.

Chapter 8 – Into The Garden

"With my soul have I desired thee in the night;
yea with my spirit within me I will seek
thee early..." (Isaiah 26:9 KJV)

My most favorite place to engage with Yahweh is in the garden of my heart. On this Sonship
journey, I have learned the importance of connecting with Yahweh at a deeper level. I spoke earlier
in this book about my relationship with Yahweh. It
has come a long way since we first got to know each
other. My purpose for sharing Chapter 8 is to encourage you to connect with Yahweh in the garden
of your heart.

The garden of your heart is the gateway of the
spirit, soul, and body. It is the love gate from which
everything flows into the three components of your
design. If we want to have a spirit, soul, and body
that will flourish, we need to connect our hearts to
the heart of Yahweh so we can be whole and want
nothing. The garden is the place where we connect
our hearts with Yahweh. It is a place that I reserve
only for Him.

My pursuit of this place came from a desire to
want to connect with Him on a personal level and
share a space of intimacy where I knew I could go
to be in His presence. The garden of my heart is

a place that represents the fruit of my interaction with Him. I can tell how well our relationship is going through the development of my garden. In my garden, I am sowing seeds to build His Kingdom and how well the garden is maintained is a spiritual representation of my interaction in the natural realm.

When I first began to engage with Yahweh in the garden of my heart, He told me He wanted me to spend two hours every morning with Him. That meant I had to get up early every morning (4:00 am - 6:00 am). To be honest, that was difficult for me. Not because I couldn't get up in the mornings, more because I like to stay up into the early morning hours, so that meant I would have to go to bed earlier so I could get some sleep at some point.

Fortunately, by this time, I was more than willing to be obedient and do what Yahweh suggested. He's just awesome and has never told me to do anything that didn't come with an amazing reward. So, I gladly purposed to meet with Him. I used my sanctified imagination to enter a door that's at the entrance of my heart. The entrance of the door represents me here in the earthly realm. When I opened the door and entered in, I was in Yahweh's Kingdom, where the garden of my heart dwells.

When I first entered the garden of my heart, it was a small space full of big overgrown leafy greenery that one would see in a jungle or tropical forest. The leaves came from the ground and were pretty big. It had beautiful lush green grass, but no colors or flowers. It was clear the garden had not been cultivated, and it had no real depth or width to it. I immediately realized that although I had been learning so much on my Sonship journey, and doing things to build the Kingdom, I had not been spending enough dedicated time with Yahweh.

This is a mistake I believe many of us make. We confuse action for the Kingdom relationship with Yahweh, Yeshua, or Ruach Hakodesh. My experience seeing the beginning of my garden is an image I will never forget. It's a reminder to me that above all things, relationship with Hashilush Hakodesh should always be first. Nothing should get in the way of that.

As I stood at the entrance of my garden, I spoke to Yahweh regarding how it should look. He told me it was my garden, and I was to cultivate it every morning. It would be a place where we could meet and talk with one another, and I could put in it whatever I wanted to. That sounded like fun to me, so I began to cultivate. Here is a description of what my garden looks like now:

When I enter the door at the southernmost point of the garden, a huge tree meets me in the front of the garden. It looks like the tree in the movie Avatar. Its branches are so high, I often stand at the highest point of the tree and look out towards the north to see the rest of my garden. Yahweh sometimes meets me under the tree, and we talk about the things that are on His mind or my mind. As I pass the tree walking north, a mountain stands in front of me. Colorful horses graze below and often walk down to the edge of the sea that stretches out to the right. The water is crystal clear, with its mouth curving in a half-circle towards the east of the garden. The sea leads to a beautiful city to the far left. The city is a brilliant, white, crystal design. To the right of the sea, there is a pathway that leads to the Garden in Eden. Yahweh and I often travel to this place by boat. To the west of the mountain, opposite the sea, the grass stretches as far as the eye can see. The horse's stables reside there, and Yahweh and I often ride our horses to the stables and beyond. He rides a white horse, and I ride a black one. On the backside of the mountain, there is a waterfall that plunges into a small lake. As I stand on the mountain, I see the entire garden. The sky is multicolored with beautiful colors. As I continue north past the mountain, there are two buildings I created. The first building is a gazebo where Yahweh and I often talk. It is open to the outside with a rectangular white crystal frame that surrounds us. Plush cushioned red benches encompass the inner frame of the gazebo, and we often talk under the sun or stars. Beyond the gazebo is a building that looks like a library. It's long and rectangular in shape that stretches south to north. The building is a transparent gold with dark maroon wood for shelving. On these shelves are journals with conversations and love letters I have written to Yahweh over the years. There are plush golden lounge chairs in the middle of the building with cocktail tables. Sometimes I sit alone and write to Yahweh, or He joins me there. I'm usually there with my lion that hangs out with me at many of the places I visit. Beyond the two buildings is a forest that extends as far as the eye can see. The scenery is absolutely beautiful with flowers, trees, and animals of all kinds. Yahweh and I often run to the edge of the forest to see the green grass continuing to grow beyond the initial boundaries.

Spending time with Yahweh, I have realized how funny He is. We have laughed together on many occasions. There are too many times to count, and too many stories to tell. I have shared a little bit with you and hope you get the idea. The intent to which I have chosen to spend time with Yahweh in the garden of my heart reflects in the effectiveness of my purpose in the natural realm and beyond. I'm hoping you will also begin to develop a garden in your heart and will make time and space to spend with Yahweh.

If you would like more information regarding how to do this, please go to our website at www. godzwow.com. There you will find a link to our podcasts. We also refer to other teachers who are on this Sonship journey and have much deeper revelations to share. Those teachers include Ian Clayton, Nancy Coen and Shannon Bates, Marios and Danielle Ellinas, Dr. Yana Sanders and Darla Fields, Grant and Sam Mahoney, Lindi Masters, Justin Abraham, Mike Parsons, and Corina Pataki to name a few.

Chapter 9 – Intercession

"For the eyes of the Lord are over the righteous,
and his ears are open unto their
prayers..." (1 Peter 3:12 NKJV)

Intercessory prayer is an integral part of the life of a believer. You hear people say, "Pray for me," or "Please pray for so and so." So much so, it's made our response to prayer requests a knee jerk reaction. We respond, "Will do." Do we take time out of our day to pray for the person or situation requested? I admit it, I have fallen into that trap and then go about my day forgetting I said it. Or, I say a quick prayer and keep moving, not setting aside quality time to address the request. Honestly, there are so many prayer requests it's hard to keep up every day.

We need to get to the point where we don't always ask others to pray for us. Instead, we should seek to gain the experiential knowledge to reach within, to the Kingdom of Yahweh, inside of us. Please, don't misunderstand me. If you are a person in desperate need of help, reach out to someone for help. However, don't make that a habit, believing that answered prayers only happen when others help. Instead, seek to grow in your spiritual maturity and get into the habit of seeking Yahweh for yourself. He has all of the answers you need, and you can hear Him easier when you have developed a relationship with Him.

I'm addressing intercessory prayer because I believe it needs to change. I believe Yahweh is changing the way we pray and the way we intercede in prayer. Prayer is defined as "spiritual communion with God." It can be done through a verbal petition or one intentionally setting one's heart on Yahweh in communion. On this Sonship journey, when I intend to pray for others, I have made more of an effort to be in spiritual communion with Yahweh. The intention is to connect to His heart to seek His desire in all situations.

After I seek out Yahweh's heart, I ask Him for the capacity to enlarge my heart, that I may have room to hold the person's request and connect with Yahweh's purpose for the outcome. Sometimes I dialogue with Yahweh about the situation, getting a better understanding of what needs to happen. Ultimately, my purpose is to connect to His heart and hold the situation in my heart until it is resolved. In that way, little words are framed from my lips. If a person hears me say, "I'm holding the situation in my heart," that's what I mean when I say that.

I love the phrase, "You can never have authority over something or someone you do not love." What that means to me is, I'm not praying for something or someone I do not love. That's very serious business for me, and I truly want to live a life of sincere prayer. As the scripture says, "Yahweh's eyes are over the righteousness, His ears are open to their prayers." (Psalms 34:15 NKJV)

The righteous are those in the right standing with Yahweh. They know His heart and are not guessing what they should do or say regarding a situation. If you want to see your prayers be effective as an intercessor, seek the heart of Yahweh in every case. It never fails.

Another way I actively involve myself in intercessory prayer is by doing communion. Communion represents the ultimate intercession made for us by the blood and sacrifice of Yeshua. Because of His sacrifice, we can partake in all that it entails and apply His victorious outcome to every situation. This can be done when speaking healing over our bodies, mending broken relationships, or accessing the treasures of heaven regarding our finances.

When you get a chance, listen to the podcast we have on the supernatural power of communion. You will hear our testimonies regarding how powerful communion is. You can do it several times a day, especially when you need the additional strength to get through a challenging situation.

Utilizing communion or expanding my love for a situation or person is now the way I engage in intercessory prayer. This type of prayer has been very effective for me and I encourage you to pursue a similar type of intercessory prayer. It is extremely powerful and has produced awesome results! I can testify...

Chapter 10 – Living In Rest

"Let us therefore fear, lest, a promise being left us of entering into rest, any of you should seem to come short of it." (Hebrews 4:11 KJV)

This Bible verse is one I believe many Christians overlook. There are so many believers walking around wounded and burdened. There is no display of peace; they are anxious and fearful. This is not Yahweh's plan for our lives. His plan for us is to live in total rest, perfect peace (shalom).

You may be asking yourself, how on earth do I get to a place of perfect peace? You mean that's possible? Well, yes. I'm here to tell you, it is possible. However, to get to a place of perfect shalom, you must do something. The Bible tells us two profound principles you need to apply in your life to achieve perfect peace.

First, we are told we should cease from doing our own works. (Hebrews 4:10 NKJV) To cease from doing our own works means to lay down our own desires and ambitions and allow Yeshua to become Lord over our lives. It means we turn the intent of our hearts towards Yeshua with the desire that our hearts be totally intertwined with His. When this happens, we no longer want to say or do anything that is contrary to the will of Yahweh, and we rest in knowing we are walking in step with Him.

Second, we are told we should labor to enter into rest. (Hebrew 4:11 NKJV) To labor into His rest means we should be intentional regarding laboring to connect to the heart of Yahweh in rest. Many people are praying for peace in their lives without knowing they already have it living inside of them. The Kingdom is as near to you as the heart that beats in your chest. It's on the inside of you, and that is where you connect to Yahweh to live in His rest. I will never forget what my mother told me. "Peace comes from within."

Perfect shalom comes from within, knowing who Hashilush Hakodesh is, and trusting They have everything you need and will give you exactly what you ask for to fulfill your destiny scroll. It doesn't matter what hardships you face. You can still live in shalom knowing you are in Him, in rest, fulfilling the desires of His heart for your life.

In previous chapters, I spoke about getting to know who Hashilush Hakodesh is. Each part of the Godhead has a different function, yet They work together as One. They function out of the same light, purpose, and heart. If this is difficult to grasp, I encourage you to spend time which each of the Godhead yourself. Practice addressing each One individually, for whatever you desire, until you have developed a way to recognize how They speak to you.

For example, in a recent situation, Hashilush Hakodesh addressed me in three different ways. As I was speaking to Them, Ruach Hakodesh said, "I will help you," then Yeshua said, "I will fight for you," and Yahweh said, "I will protect you." It was awesome for me to know how They see Their role in my life. Praise Yahweh! Who has anything to fear when the Godhead tells you what They will do for you? I have developed such a relationship with Hashilush Hakodesh that I have no doubt every question I have will be answered.

In the past, this wasn't always the case. Eventually, I had to make a decision to be intentional about getting to know Them. I remember trying to get all of the noise in my head to be quiet. I spent one hour, doing my best to keep still and silence the noise in my head so I could hear His voice. After one hour, I heard Yahweh say, "You have a lot to learn."

I remember thinking, "Wow, that's what I get to hear after being quiet for one hour?" However, what Yahweh said was absolutely true. At that time, I thought I knew so much about spiritual matters. The truth was I was just beginning, and I had to do more to clear the static I heard when I purposed to be still.

So, I decided to fast to help quiet the static in my mind. I fasted food, electronics, and purposed to speak words that only encompassed life. I spent hours speaking in tongues and spent several days at a time in solitude. I did see things begin to change in my spiritual journey, and my mind was clearer but knew I needed to do more.

Significant breakthrough came when I began

to do communion several times a day on a regular basis. It gave me the ability to connect with Hashilush Hakodesh like never before and opened up a doorway to another realm. Stepping into the Throne of Grace and connecting with Yahweh by participating in communion changed me from the inside out. I literally felt a change in my body, soul, and spirit. My spirit man developed the strength needed to command my soul to conform to the government of Yahweh's Kingdom.

It has been a process, but well worth the sacrifice. The relationship I have with Hashilush Hakodesh cannot be traded for anything in existence. I'm just that committed.

I hope you will commit yourself to encounter Hashilush Hakodesh in a life-changing way. That you may know the depth, breadth, and height of who you are and what your function is on earth and in heaven.

A Prayer

"May the love of Yahweh pour over you like a never-ending flood. May you be totally immersed and encompassed with what it means to know the love He has for you. And may the love He has for you shine through you and touch everyone that you meet. For His love for us takes us into eternity and beyond..."

About Author

Nina L. Hayden is an attorney, professor, and politician who has co-founded Godzwow, Inc., Godzwow Publications, Inc., and Shaar Lamed in Pinellas County, Florida. She is passionate about the study of the Bible as it relates to engaging in Kingdom mysteries. She believes it is possible to mature in your spiritual journey by building the garden of your heart.

In this book, Nina reveals her relational connection with Father, Son, and Holy Spirit. "The Bible is a love letter written as an invitation to learn how the Father's heart works, but it doesn't reveal the whole entirety of who God is. If we want to know Father, Son, and Holy Spirit at a deeper level, we must personally encounter who They are as Beings." She goes on further to state, "Through the word made flesh, the invitation is given to come, reason, commune, and walk with God."

Godzwow, Inc. is a business with a ministry focus. Their various products and services are designed to engage you with the heart of Yahweh (YHVH) and create a culture of Heaven on Earth. Through Nina's book, you are invited to join this incredible journey, engage and interact with Father God, today and indeed beyond.

Published by

Godzwow Publications, Inc.

GODZWOW
Publications

www.godzwowpublications.com